A PUERTO RICO TRAVEL GUIDE BOOK

2023

For Complete Family Friendly Puerto Rico Experience And All You Need To Know

Jette Florence

Copyright © 2023 by **Jette Florence**

Table Of Contents

Discovering Puerto Rico's Enchanting Isle Where Adventure And Serenity Meet

When looking for a place with all the enabling factors to make you feel serene all through your vacation and coming home feeling refreshed, Puerto Rico is that place.

With a thriving culture, stunning natural surroundings, and friendly people that weave together to provide extraordinary experience, Puerto Rico, which is tucked away in the Caribbean, calls to you with its appeal and promises a trip that goes beyond the usual and explores the remarkable.

Prepare to be carried away on an exciting adventure into a world of contrasts and harmonies as you flip the pages of this painstakingly written tour guide.

Puerto Rico captivates all of your senses, giving you a symphony of feelings and experiences that will last long after your departure, from the frenetic rhythms of salsa dancing in the cobblestone alleyways of Old San Juan to the calming lullaby of waves caressing beautiful, sandy beaches.

- ## Unlock Treasures On The Island.

This tour will reveal the undiscovered treasures that characterize Puerto Rico's essence in addition to the famous sites and well-traveled routes. Explore verdant jungles where small coqus and colorful parrots sing you beneath a canopy of old trees.

Uncover the mysteries of venerable strongholds that have stood as stoic witnesses to the island's turbulent past and are protecting tales of tenacity and freedom.

...Food, Food, Food!
Explore the gastronomic delights that are around every corner, from upscale eateries that combine traditional flavors with contemporary flair to roadside stands selling juicy alcapurrias and savory mofongo.

Get ready to go off on a culinary excursion that will satisfy both your taste senses and your heart.

- ## Experience Thrill And Calm In A Perfect Balance

Puerto Rico provides a wide range of activities to fulfill the desires of any tourist, whether you are an adrenaline addict looking for world-class waves to surf or a peace seeker looking for solitude in remote coves.

You can enjoy the grandeur of golden sunsets that tint the sky in shades of orange and pink, snorkel through clear seas to see fascinating marine life, walk deep into

El Yunque National Forest to see cascading waterfalls, or just sit back and take it all in.

● It Is A Connections Journey

Puerto Rico welcomes you to engage with its people, experience their kindness, and get fully immersed in its rich traditions. It is more than simply a place to visit.

Here, you'd discover the vivacious attitude of the inhabitants as they celebrate life via vivid and lively festivals. Talk to people who speak other languages, and you will develop lifelong friendships.

● Obtain Your Passport to Paradise Now

Your go-to travel companion, this thorough Puerto Rico travel guide has been meticulously compiled to provide you all the information, insider knowledge, and itinerary inspiration you need to plan an amazing trip.

Puerto Rico extends a warm welcome to all travelers, whether they are lone adventurers seeking self-discovery, a couple seeking love, or a family seeking priceless memories.

Therefore, browse these pages and let your imagination soar. Puerto Rico is waiting for you when you get there, eager to paint your heart with hues you never knew existed.

Accept the challenge, savor the peace, and let the charm of this tropical haven make a lasting impression on your spirit. Your journey across Puerto Rico has started!

Chapter 1

Travel Guide To Puerto Rico

Welcome to Puerto Rico, a lush haven tucked deep within the Caribbean Sea. Puerto Rico, also referred to as the *"Island of Enchantment,"* is a mesmerizing location that offers a rich fusion of history, culture, and natural beauty.

Every traveler, whether they enjoy the beach, outdoor activities, or history, will find something unique in Puerto Rico.

An Overview of Puerto Rico's Geography

Puerto Rico is a US territory that is not incorporated and is situated in the northeastern Caribbean. The island is the smallest of the Greater Antilles, being around 100 miles long and 35 miles wide.

The main island of Puerto Rico is bordered by various smaller islands, such as Culebra and Vieques, each of which has an own beauty.

The geography of the island is varied, with dense rainforests, rocky mountains, and fine golden sand beaches. One of the island's natural wonders, El Yunque National Forest is a tropical rainforest that draws tourists with its breathtaking waterfalls, varied fauna, and hiking paths.

History and Cultural Heritage

The indigenous Tano people, Spanish colonists, African slaves, and several other cultural influences have all contributed to the fascinating fabric of Puerto Rico's past.

The Taino people lived on the island for a long time until Christopher Columbus claimed it in 1493 for Spain. Puerto Rico was a crucial military and commercial outpost for the Spanish Empire for many years.

The architecture of the island still bears the influence of Spanish colonialism, particularly in Old San Juan, the capital city's historic center.

Visitors are transported back in time by cobblestone walkways, vibrant houses with elaborate balconies, and imposing fortresses like El Morro and San Cristobal. Old San Juan is now a bustling center for dining, shopping, and cultural events as well as a UNESCO World Heritage Site.

Unique Features and Attractions

The Bioluminescent Bays

Mosquito Bay in Vieques, Laguna Grande in Fajardo, and La Parguera in Lajas are the three bioluminescent bays found in Puerto Rico.

These amazing natural phenomena are filled with microorganisms that give off a mystical blue-green glow at night, giving kayakers and other nighttime travelers a unique experience.

Flamenco Beach

Flamenco Beach, which lies on the island of Culebra, is frequently cited as one of the most stunning beaches in the world.

Its picture-perfect setting is ideal for swimming, snorkeling, and simply soaking up the sun thanks to its crystal-clear waters, spotless white beach, and lush green hills.

Camuy River Cave Park

Boasting one of the largest cave systems in the world, the Camuy River Cave Park will enthrall nature lovers. Investigate the fascinating underground features, which include large caves, stalactites, and an underground river that meanders through the underground setting.

Festivals and Music

Puerto Ricans have a robust cultural past, which is celebrated via various festivals. During events like the San Sebastián Street Festival and the Fiestas de la Calle San Sebastián.

The atmosphere is infused with an addictive energy thanks to the island's music, which includes salsa, reggaeton, and bombay plena.

Best Of Time To Visit Puerto Rico

Puerto Rico's dry season, which lasts from December to April, is the ideal time to visit. With mild temperatures and reduced humidity levels, this time of year has the most pleasant weather, making it the best for sightseeing and outdoor activities.

It is vital to remember that the winter months are peak travel season, so plan on more people and more expensive accommodations.

Consider going between May and November, which are the shoulder seasons, for a more affordable and less crowded experience.

Even if there may be a few rain showers here and there, the island is still very sunny throughout these months, giving you the chance to appreciate it without the crowds of people.

Chapter 2

Planning Your Trip

Requirements for Travel Document and Visa

Make sure you have all the required travel paperwork before starting your trip to Puerto Rico. U.S. citizens do not require a passport to travel to Puerto Rico because it is a U.S. territory.

Entry requires a government-issued photo ID, such as a driver's license. However, it is always a good idea to confirm any recent changes to the rules and prerequisites for travel before you depart.

The same visa policies that apply to visitors to any other U.S. location also apply to foreign visitors arriving from America. Make sure you have a current visa if you are a non-citizen living in the United States, and check with your embassy or consulate to see if there are any other conditions for visiting Puerto Rico.

Picking the Best Travel Period

Due to its tropical warmth, Puerto Rico is a popular vacation spot all year round. The ideal time to travel, however, will depend on your interests and the experiences you hope to have while there.

High Season (December to April)
Travelers seeking to escape chilly regions flock to this region at this time. You should anticipate slightly higher costs and more people, but you can also look forward to more beautiful weather and little rain.

Low Season (May to November)
While the low season can be hotter and more likely to rain, it also has less visitors and less expensive lodging options. This might be the best time to go if you want to find affordable options and have a more relaxing experience.

Budgeting and Money Matters

To make the most of your holiday, you must set a budget for your trip to Puerto Rico. Puerto Rico is typically less expensive than several other Caribbean locations, however rates can change based on your vacation preferences and style.

Accommodations
Season and location can affect how much a hotel costs. Consider staying in guesthouses, hostels, or vacation rentals to save money. There are also affordable and upscale accommodations available.

Public transportation
Public transportation, including cabs and buses, is widely available in Puerto Rico. If you want greater freedom to explore the island thoroughly, you should rent a car. If you decide to take this route, plan on paying for gas, tolls, and parking.

Food & Dining
Puerto Rico has a wide variety of delectable eateries, from fine dining to street food. While eating at neighborhood restaurants and food trucks can be inexpensive, fancy dining will cost more money.

Activities & Attractions
Many of Puerto Rico's attractions, like its beaches, wildlife preserves, and historic sites, are cost-free or only need a small entrance fee. Spend money on

any particular experiences you want to have, such as excursions, trips, or water sports.

Puerto Rico Travel Essentials

Your trip to the island will be comfortable and pleasurable if you bring the correct items with you. The following are some items you might want to bring:

1. **Warm-weather attire** that is light and breathable, such as swimwear and beach cover-ups.

2. **Sunscreen, eyewear, and a hat** with a wide brim to shield oneself from the intense tropical sun.

3. **Bug spray**, especially if you intend to visit undeveloped areas.

4. **Comfy walking shoes or sandals** for beach activities and sightseeing.

5. **A water bottle** that you may reuse to stay hydrated while on your trips.

6. **A travel adaptor and a charger** for your electronic gadgets, as Puerto Rico utilizes the same power outlets as the United States.

7. **A fundamental first-aid kit** and any essential drugs.

8. **A tiny waterproof case or bag** for the beach that you can use to store your phone and other belongings.

9. Pack a small umbrella or raincoat, especially if you are traveling during a wet season.

10. This Travel guide as a Spanish phrasebook or language app, as learning some fundamental Spanish phrases can be useful and appreciated even though many locals understand English.

Chapter 3

Getting to Puerto Rico

In this chapter, we will explore the various ways to get to Puerto Rico from America, including air travel, cruises, and land transportation options.

Airports And Transportation Options

Puerto Rico is well-connected by air, and visitors can choose from several airports to reach the island. The two major airports are:

The Luis Muñoz Marín International Airport (SJU): Located in the capital city of San Juan, SJU is the primary international gateway to Puerto Rico. It serves as a hub for various airlines and offers numerous domestic and international flight options.

The Rafael Hernández Airport (BQN): Situated in Aguadilla on the island's northwest coast, BQN provides an alternative option for international travelers, especially those coming from the eastern parts of the United States.

Domestic And International Flights

Domestic Flights

Traveling to Puerto Rico from different parts of the United States is convenient, with many major airlines offering direct flights to SJU from cities such as Miami, New York, Atlanta, and Orlando, among others.

Flight durations vary depending on the departure city, but most domestic flights take between 2 to 4 hours to reach the island.

International Flights

Visitors from around the world can easily access Puerto Rico through direct international flights to SJU. Many airlines operate routes from Canada, Europe, and South America, making it a well-connected destination.

Travelers can also find indirect flights with layovers in major U.S. cities to reach Puerto Rico.

Cruises And Sea Travel

For a unique and leisurely way to reach Puerto Rico, consider embarking on a cruise. Several cruise lines offer itineraries that include the island as a port of call. San Juan, in particular, is a popular cruise port and serves as a starting or ending point for many Caribbean cruise journeys.

Cruise passengers get to enjoy stunning views of the island as they approach the port. Moreover, they have the opportunity to explore various attractions and activities on the island during their stopover.

Popular cruise lines that frequent Puerto Rico include Royal Caribbean, Carnival Cruise Line, and Norwegian Cruise Line, among others.

Routes For Traveling To Puerto Rico By Land

While it's not possible to drive to Puerto Rico from the United States mainland due to the Caribbean Sea in between, visitors from nearby islands and territories have the option of traveling by ferry or private boat. The most common routes are:

From the Dominican Republic

Ferries operate between Santo Domingo, the capital of the Dominican Republic, and San Juan, Puerto Rico. The journey takes approximately 12-14 hours, and travelers can bring their vehicles along.

From the U.S. Virgin Islands

Ferries connect St. Thomas and St. Croix, part of the U.S. Virgin Islands, to San Juan, Puerto Rico. The travel time varies depending on the specific route, but it generally takes a few hours.

Keep in mind that the availability of ferry services and their schedules may change, so it's essential to check in advance and plan accordingly.

With its excellent air connectivity, cruise options, and ferry services from nearby islands, getting to Puerto Rico is relatively easy and offers diverse travel experiences. Whether you choose to fly directly into the bustling capital of San Juan or embark on a relaxing cruise adventure, the enchanting island of Puerto Rico is sure to captivate you with its warmth, beauty, and vibrant culture.

Chapter 4

Exploring San Juan, The Capital

The intriguing city of San Juan, the capital of Puerto Rico, successfully combines a long past with a contemporary flair. San Juan offers a variety of experiences for visitors, from its antique cobblestone streets to its energetic districts.

This chapter will explore the many elements of this wonderful city, including Old San Juan, the world-famous fortifications of El Morro and Castillo San Cristobal, the vibrant Santurce neighborhood, and San Juan's contemporary side.

Learning About The Old San Juan

The UNESCO World Heritage Site of Old San Juan provides a reminder of the city's colonial past. You will get a sense of time travel as soon as you enter its winding cobblestone streets.

The buildings' ornate wrought-iron balconies and colorful exterior give off an old-world elegance. Numerous must-see attractions may be found here, and the history is evident wherever you turn:

Castillo San Felipe del Morro (El Morro)
The 16th-century stronghold known as El Morro is boldly perched on a rocky outcropping with a view of the Atlantic Ocean.

Its imposing fortifications and advantageous location were essential in keeping the city safe from attacks. Enjoy a leisurely stroll along the fortress walls while taking in expansive sea views.

Discover the labyrinth of tunnels, dungeons, and barracks inside to gain insight into the lives of the soldiers that once guarded the city.

Another impressive fortification worth investigating is Castillo San Cristobal, which is connected to El Morro by a network of tunnels.

This enormous 18th-century building, which was formerly a military bastion, provides stunning views of the town. Do not overlook the sentry boxes, a distinctive feature of Spanish colonial fortifications that were employed for signaling and observation.

Visiting Castillo San Cristobal and El Morro

El Morro and Castillo San Cristobal both play significant roles in the history of Puerto Rico and offer unique insights into the city's tactical defense system.

You will be transported into a world of warfare, artillery, and architectural marvels when you explore these fortifications. Here are some useful pointers for your trip:

Visiting Times
El Morro and Castillo San Cristobal are open to visitors every day, excluding some federal holidays. For the most recent opening times and any upcoming activities, visit the official website.

Guided Tours
To obtain a deeper grasp of the historical significance and architectural characteristics of these fortifications, think about taking a guided tour.

Safety Tips

Wear sunscreen, a hat, and comfortable shoes because much of the exploring will take place outside. You should also carry a water bottle to stay hydrated.

Enjoying the Vibrant Santurce District

Santurce is a vibrant area in San Juan renowned for its arts, culture, and upbeat ambiance. You can find a wide variety of street art, galleries, and entertainment alternatives here, where creativity is in vogue.

Visit Santurce for a day and take in the following highlights:

Museo de Arte de Puerto Rico

This gallery houses artwork from the 17th century to contemporary pieces, making it a veritable treasure trove of Puerto Rican art.

Enjoy the various art exhibitions and collections that showcase the island's rich cultural and historical legacy.

La Placita de Santurce

As dusk falls, La Placita erupts with lively bars, eateries, and live music. Join the locals for an entertaining evening of dancing, delectable Puerto Rican food, and welcoming island friendliness.

Experiencing Modern San Juan

San Juan has a booming modern side with upmarket dining, shopping, and entertainment opportunities in addition to its historic appeal. Here are some contemporary sights to see:

Condado Beach
This well-known city beach is ideal for recreation in the water. After spending the day swimming, sunbathing, or participating in water sports, take a trip down Ashford Avenue to locate chic shops and eateries.

La Ventana al Mar, often known as "The Window to the Sea," is a picturesque location with a lovely park for picnics and leisurely strolls.

Puerto Rico Convention Center District
Throughout the year, this area is home to a number of events, conventions, and trade exhibits. To find out if there are any intriguing events that coincide with your visit, check the event calendar.

As you stroll through contemporary San Juan, you will see how the city dynamically blends traditional and modern influences, producing a singular experience that appeals to a wide range of interests.

Travelers can experience an unforgettably rich trip through time and culture in San Juan thanks to its unique history, energetic neighborhoods, and cutting-edge services. Accept the variety of experiences the city has to offer and get lost in the allure and beauty of the capital of Puerto Rico.

Chapter 5

Island-Hopping Adventures

This is Chapter 5 of your travel guide to Puerto Rico. We will take you on an incredible voyage through Puerto Rico's alluring island-hopping experiences in this chapter.

During our exploration of four gorgeous islands, each with its own special charm and attractiveness, we will uncover the hidden gems of this Caribbean paradise.

Prepare to be mesmerized by the bioluminescent bays, immaculate beaches, vibrant marine life, and historical sites that these island experiences have in store for you.

Vieques' Pristine Beaches and Bioluminescent Bay

A remarkable natural wonder, Vieques is a little island about eight miles off the eastern coast of Puerto Rico. The Bioluminescent Bay, sometimes referred to as Mosquito Bay, is one of its most well-known attractions. Due to the presence of microscopic dinoflagellates, the bay's waters take on an unreal, brilliant blue tint when the sun sets.

The wonderful experience of kayaking through this bioluminescent wonderland will stay with you forever.

In addition to the captivating bay, Vieques is home to some of the Caribbean's most pristine and remote beaches. You should definitely stop by Sun Bay and Navio Beach, where you may relax on smooth, white beaches and go swimming in crystal-clear water.

The Vieques National Wildlife Refuge's rich flora and fauna, where wild horses can wander freely and birdwatching chances abound, will appeal to nature lovers.

Flamenco Beach and Snorkeling Spots on Culebra

Another lovely island off the coast of Puerto Rico is Culebra, which is known for its stunning Flamenco Beach. This crescent-shaped beach's turquoise waters and fine white sand are among the best in the world. It is perfect for swimming and picnicking because to the tranquil waters, and the verdant hills make for excellent photo locations.

The several snorkeling locations on Culebra, including Tamarindo and Melones Beach, will please divers.

Put on your snorkeling equipment and explore the fascinating underwater world of vivid coral reefs filled with marine life, including tropical fish, rays, and, if you are lucky, sea turtles.

Untouched Nature And A Diving Paradise On Mona Island

A true adventurer's paradise, Mona Island is a secluded and unpopulated nature reserve situated between Puerto Rico and the Dominican Republic.

This undiscovered treasure offers a pristine and unspoiled natural setting and is reachable only by boat. Visitors are urged to abide by preservation requirements in order to safeguard the area's delicate ecosystem despite the fact that hiking and exploration are ideal on its difficult terrain.

Divers will find Mona Island to be a very exceptional location. There is a wealth of marine life in the area's seas, including spectacular coral formations, playful dolphins, and secretive sharks.

Do not pass up the chance to explore the underwater tunnels and caverns if you are a qualified diver; they give an extra element of adventure to your diving experience.

The Fort and Wildlife Reserve At Isla De Cabras

Isla de Cabras (Goat Island), which is close to the capital San Juan, offers a blend of history and nature. The island is home to Fort San Juan de la Cruz, a 17th-century Spanish fortification also known as El Cauelo.

Discover the fort's ruins, which are a reminder of the island's colonial past, and take in the expansive views of San Juan Bay and the skyline of the city.

Isla de Cabras is a wonderful location for birdwatchers and other environment lovers because it is also a recognized wildlife reserve. Pelicans and herons are among the bird species that flock to the island's coastal regions. Take a leisurely stroll down the shore while keeping an eye out for the variety of marine life that calls the area's waters home.

Take back with you the memories of Puerto Rico's spectacular natural beauty, illuminating history, and welcoming people as you wrap up your island-hopping excursions there.

Every traveler may find something to do in Puerto Rico's islands, whether they want to unwind on pristine beaches, explore historical sites, or go diving. Prepare to immerse yourself in the vivid culture and mesmerizing scenery that this wonderful voyage has in store for you!

Chapter 6

Delightful Cuisine and Local Food

Puerto Rico is renowned for its delectable cuisine, which combines Taino, Spanish, and African elements.

Every food enthusiast will have a wonderful experience with the island's cuisine, which features both traditional recipes that have been passed down through the years and modern fusion innovations.

The traditional foods and flavors of Puerto Rico, must-try eateries in San Juan, regional food markets, and the enticing world of street food and snacks will all be covered in this chapter.

Traditional Puerto Rican Dishes and Flavors

Mofongo
Mofongo is a traditional Puerto Rican cuisine made with mashed green plantains and chicharrón, which is a type of pork crackling. This filling and savory

dish is sometimes offered with the option of chicken, shrimp, or pork as the meat.

Arroz with Gandules
A traditional dish served at celebrations, Arroz con Gandules is a fragrant rice dish prepared with pigeon peas, sofrito (a mixture of onions, garlic, peppers, and herbs), and frequently served with succulent slices of pork.

Lechón
The roasted pig that Puerto Ricans are so proud of is called as lechón. Adobo is used to season the whole pig before it is slow-roasted on a spit until the skin is crispy and the meat is luscious and tender.

Bacalaitos
Bacalaitos are salty codfish fritters cooked from a batter of flour, spice, and bacalao (salted cod). On the entire island, people love to snack on these crunchy treats.

Alcapurrias
Popular Puerto Rican street food, these deep-fried fritters are usually stuffed with seasoned beef and prepared from a mixture of green bananas, yauta (taro root), and ground meat.

Restaurants In San Juan You Must Try

Jose Enrique

Jose Enrique, a well regarded restaurant serving modern Puerto Rican cuisine with an emphasis on locally produced ingredients, is situated in the lively district of Santurce. Their menu offers imaginative takes on classic foods, and the setting is cozy and welcoming.

La Casita Blanca

Visit this quaint restaurant in San Juan to experience the true flavors of Puerto Rico. This eatery, which is well-known for its hearty fare and welcoming ambiance, lets customers experience the true flavor of Puerto Rican comfort food.

Marmalade

Marmalade is a great option for anyone looking for a fine-dining experience that places a focus on regional ingredients and gourmet flair. Their creative tasting menus incorporate inspirations from around the world while honoring the island's culinary tradition.

Visiting Local Food Markets

Mercado de Santurce

Santurce's busy market is a foodie's dream come true. Local coffee, artisanal cheeses, fresh veggies, and wholesome snacks are all available here. It is a great place to experience regional cuisine and talk to welcoming merchants.

Rio Piedras' Plaza del Mercado

This bustling market in Rio Piedras is home to a wide selection of tropical fruits, herbs, and spices as well as a plethora of street food vendors. It is a great site to get a sense of Puerto Rican culture through its sights, music, and cuisine.

Snacks And Street Food

Piones Kiosks

Just east of San Juan, along the picturesque Piones Road, you will find a number of kiosks selling mouthwatering foods such as alcapurrias, bacalaitos, and empanadillas. This street food experience is made even more charming by its beachside location.

Chinchorreo excursion

Hire a car and go on an excursion known as a "chinchorreo," during which you visit several roadside food stands and sample regional specialties. This is a genuine way to experience the island's wide variety of street food options.

Do not forget to enjoy every morsel of the delicious food Puerto Rico has to offer. The island's flavors will stay with you long after you leave, when you indulge in street food, visit local markets, or eat at a fine dining establishment.

Chapter 7

Outdoor activities and Adventure

For vacationers looking for an adrenaline rush and a personal touch with nature, Puerto Rico offers a wide variety of outdoor and adventure sports. This chapter will walk you through some of the most fascinating things the island has to offer, from beautiful rainforests to exhilarating water sports.

Walking The El Yunque National Forest

Hikers and wildlife lovers alike should travel to El Yunque National Forest, also called the Caribbean National Forest.

Within the United States National Forest System, this tropical rainforest is the only one of its kind and is home to a staggering variety of flora and fauna. *The following are some highlights and advice for your hike in El Yunque:*

El Yunque has trails that are appropriate for hikers of all skill levels, from novices to seasoned trail runners. The La Mina Falls Trail, Big Tree Trail, and El Yunque Trail are a few well-liked paths that each provide distinctive experiences and breath-taking scenery.

The La Mina Falls
The La Mina Falls are one of El Yunque's most popular destinations. Many visitors can access the falls thanks to the very simple trail that leads there. A nice swim in the waterfall's chilly waters is the hike's reward after a long day of walking.

Safety Advice
It is important to be ready for shifting weather conditions when hiking in El Yunque. Bring enough water, put on comfy hiking shoes, and use bug repellant. Additionally, exercise caution during and after periods of heavy rain since trails may become slick.

Canopy Tours And Ziplining

Ziplining and canopy tours offer an amazing opportunity to discover Puerto Rico's rich surroundings from above for tourists looking for an adrenaline-packed adventure.

The island has a number of zipline parks that guarantee unique experiences and breath-taking aerial views:

Toro Verde Nature Adventure Park
Toro Verde, a popular zipline park on the island, is situated near Orocovis. One of the longest and fastest ziplines in the world, "The Beast," is their standout attraction. It is about a mile long and reaches astounding speeds.

Zip lining in the midst of Nature
You will get a rare chance to view Puerto Rico's diverse flora and animals from a completely different perspective as you soar over the treetops.

Safety and Requirements
Before starting a ziplining excursion, make sure you have the required safety gear and are following the advice of knowledgeable instructors. It is important to double verify the requirements in advance because there may be age and weight limits.

Water Sports And Surfing

Puerto Rico is a surfer's and water sports enthusiast's dream with its warm tropical waters and reliable waves. The island includes surf places and aquatic activities for everyone, whether you are a pro surfer or a beginner trying to catch your first wave:

Rincon

Rincon boasts world-class surfing conditions and is referred to be the "Caribbean's Surf Capital." The surges are particularly noticeable in the winter and draw surfers from all around the world.

Surf Schools

If you have never surfed before, do not be alarmed! All throughout the island, there are numerous surf schools and instructors who provide instruction for beginners of all ages.

Other Water Sports

Puerto Rico provides a variety of water activities in addition to surfing, including paddleboarding, snorkeling, scuba diving, and jet skiing. These activities are made even more delightful by the clean seas and a variety of marine life.

Cavern And Cave Exploration In Puerto Rico

A unique network of tunnels and caves may be found on the island of Puerto Rico, providing an opportunity to explore the mysterious underworld. The following noteworthy caverns and caves should be on your itinerary:

Rio Camuy Cave Park

This park, which is in the municipality of Camuy, has a sizable network of limestone caves. The area's geological structures and history can be learned while taking a trip of some of the remarkable caverns.

Cueva Ventana

Cueva Ventana, which translates as "Window Cave," provides a distinctive experience. Visitors are rewarded with a spectacular view of the surrounding terrain through a natural "window" in the cave after a little stroll.

Safety And Conservation

It is crucial to abide by any safety instructions given by guides and authorities while exploring caverns. In order to protect these fragile landscapes for future generations, conservation activities are also essential.

Chapter 8

Embracing The Culture

With its rich history, lively traditions, and welcoming people, Puerto Rico is a cultural haven that enchants visitors. This chapter will examine the fundamental elements of Puerto Rican culture and the different ways visitors can fully experience the island's rich history.

Traditional Holidays And Festivities

Participating in Puerto Rico's customary festivals and celebrations is one of the best ways to explore the island's culture. The island comes alive all year long with vibrant events that highlight its many cultural influences. Among the festivals that are a must-attend are:

Fiesta de la Calle San Sebastián

Old San Juan's cobblestone alleys comes alive in January for San Juan's Fiesta de la Calle San Sebastián, a bustling street festival with live entertainment, cuisine, and specialty goods. It is the ideal chance to experience the vigor and passion of Puerto Rican music and dancing styles like Bomba and Plena.

Ponce Carnival
The Ponce Carnival, which takes place in February, is a lavish spectacle of parades, ornate costumes, and upbeat music. The carnival, which has roots in both African and Spanish customs, provides a special window into Puerto Rico's rich cultural diversity.

Fiestas de la Calle San Felipe
This festival honors the town's patron saint with religious processions, street cuisine, live music, and traditional dances and is held in the town of Arecibo in May.

Latin Music Scene And Salsa

Puerto Rico's robust salsa and Latin music scene is a must-experience during any visit. Salsa originated on the island, and there are several clubs, bars, and live music venues where you can dance the night away.

Do not be afraid to learn some salsa moves and join the natives on the dance floor, whether you are an expert dancer or a beginner. La Placita de Santurce and Nuyorican Café are well known in San Juan for their energetic ambiance and top-notch music.

Locally Made Crafts

Investigate the local arts and crafts scene to fully experience Puerto Rico's unique creativity.

A variety of exquisitely created products, including as vibrant paintings, handmade pottery, elaborate wood carvings, and traditional vejigante masks, may be found in artisan markets and galleries.

The city of Ponce has an amazing art museum and art walks that feature the creations of both local and foreign artists, while the village of Loiza is well known for its Afro-Caribbean craftsmanship.

Discovering Taino Heritage

Understanding Puerto Rico's indigenous ancestry is crucial to fully comprehending the island's culture. Before the Spanish arrived, the Taino people lived on the island permanently.

Although colonization caused the Taino culture serious problems, its impact may still be seen in Puerto Rican traditions, language, and art.

Learn about Taino spirituality and culture by visiting the Caguana Indigenous Ceremonial Park in Utuado, where you may examine historic petroglyphs. The Tibes Indigenous Ceremonial Center in Ponce also provides information on the past and way of life of the Taino people.

Numerous cultural institutions and museums all around the island offer educational exhibitions and programs that highlight Taino heritage, ensuring that their legacy is preserved and valued.

Travelers can develop a greater understanding of Puerto Rico's uniqueness and make priceless memories of their wonderful visit by embracing the island's festivals, music, arts, and Taino heritage.

Chapter 9

Wellness And Relaxation

There are many chances for relaxation and wellness in Puerto Rico, making it more than just a place for exploration and adventure.

The island offers something to offer for every tourist looking to relax and revitalize, whether they are looking for a serene beach getaway, an opulent spa retreat, or a life-changing yoga experience.

Top Beach Destinations

Flamenco Beach, Culebra Island
Flamenco Beach consistently makes lists of the most beautiful beaches in the world, and it is not hard to understand why.

A picture-perfect scene for leisure is created by the fine, white-powder sand and the turquoise, crystal-clear waters. This calm beach is a great place to relax while taking in the lovely sounds of the waves, swim, and sunbathe.

Luquillo Beach, Luquillo

Known as Puerto Rico's "Sun Capital," Luquillo Beach is a well-liked local hangout for both locals and tourists. It gives the ideal setting for a relaxed day by the shore with its calm waves and lush surrounding palm palms.

Travelers can savor authentic Puerto Rican cuisines at a number of stalls along the beach that provide great regional fare.

Playa Sucia, Cabo Rojo

Playa Sucia is a more remote and off-the-beaten-path beach that is situated in the southwest of the island. This lovely beach offers a tranquil ambiance and is surrounded by cliffs and natural scenery, making it the perfect place for a relaxing holiday.

Luxury Resorts And Spas

Dorado Beach, a Ritz-Carlton Reserve, Dorado

This upscale resort fuses elegance, luxury, and unmatched natural beauty. Dorado Beach, which is located on a former coconut plantation, provides visitors a secluded and private experience.

A renowned spa offering a variety of soothing treatments and therapies is one of the resort's top-notch amenities.

St. Regis Bahia Beach Resort, Rio Grande

The St. Regis Bahia Beach Resort is a serene retreat nestled between a lush national forest and a fine beach. The hotel has a Remède Spa where visitors can enjoy individualized treatments and unwind in a serene setting.

Yoga Retreats and Meditation Centers

The Yoga Loft, San Juan

The Yoga Loft is a well-liked gathering place for residents and tourists looking for yoga sessions and health programs. It is located in the center of San Juan.

The center provides a variety of yoga classes, meditation sessions, and holistic activities to improve emotional and physical health.

Casa Grande Mountain Retreat, Utuado

Casa Grande Mountain Retreat provides a tranquil setting for yoga retreats and spiritual inquiry. It is surrounded by the breathtaking mountains of Utuado. In order to provide a comprehensive wellness experience, the retreat center conducts yoga sessions, mindfulness programs, and hiking trips.

Finding Inner Peace In Puerto Rico

El Yunque National Forest, Rio Grande

El Yunque is a biodiverse jungle as well as a haven of unspoiled tranquility. It may be really calming to lose yourself in the lush foliage and tranquil sounds of nature; it is the ideal way to reconnect with yourself and achieve inner peace.

Vieques and Fajardo, bioluminescent bays

Vieques and Fajardo are home to some of the most breathtaking bioluminescent bays in the entire globe.

An fascinating and peaceful experience can be had by participating in a guided kayak tour on a moonless night, which shows the magical glow of the bioluminescent organisms in the water.

Chapter 10

Giving Back And Sustainable Travel

In addition to being a stunning location, Puerto Rico offers visitors the chance to practice sustainability and give back to the area's locals and environment.

Visitors can have a positive impact on the island by using eco-friendly travel strategies, aiding neighborhood projects, and booking eco-friendly lodging.

This chapter will guide you on how to travel ethically and support the protection of Puerto Rico's natural and cultural wonders.

Responsible Travel Practices

You may do a number of things as a responsible traveler to lessen your influence on Puerto Rico's fragile ecological and cultural heritage:

Reduce Waste
To avoid single-use plastic items, carry a reusable water bottle, shopping bag, and utensils. Use recycling bins properly; there are plenty of them in Puerto Rico.

Engage In Nature Protection Practices
A variety of plants and animals, some of which are endangered, can be found on Puerto Rico. Avoid disturbing animals or destroying their habitats. Follow the designated routes and refrain from plucking flowers or coral reefs.

Promote Local Business
To actively promote the island's economy, patronize locally owned shops, eateries, and craft markets. Interact culturally with the locals and be respectful of their traditions.

Shopping for souvenirs mindfully
Steer clear of items created from threatened or illegally harvested species. Instead, choose genuine regional products that highlight Puerto Rico's vibrant culture.

Eco-Friendly Accommodations

On the island, a number of lodgings are dedicated to minimizing their environmental impact. Think about staying at green lodges, hotels, or inns that have adopted sustainable practices:

Energy conservation
Seek out lodgings that power their facilities with sustainable energy sources like solar or wind turbines.

Water Management
Pick locations with water conservation features like low-flow toilets and rainwater collection systems.

Recycling and Waste Reduction
Look for accommodations that place a high priority on recycling and have procedures in place to reduce waste production.

Environmental Certifications
To demonstrate their dedication to sustainability, some hotels may hold certifications like LEED (Leadership in Energy and Environmental Design) or the Green Key eco-label.

Volunteer Works In Puerto Rico

If you wish to have a more immediate influence when you are there, think about helping Puerto Rico with its conservation initiatives by volunteering:

Beach Clean-ups

Beach clean-ups are organized by a number of groups to safeguard the beauty of the coastline and marine life. Attend one of these events while you are here.

Reforestation Projects

Participate in tree-planting campaigns to preserve and restore Puerto Rico's verdant forests.

Marine Conservation

Participate in initiatives like the preservation of sea turtles or the repair of coral reefs.

Community Development

Assist groups that work on community development initiatives like enhancing infrastructure, health, and education.

Supporting Local Communities and Conservation Efforts

Several community-based projects and conservation groups in Puerto Rico seek support from visitors:

Donations
Contribute to neighborhood nonprofits and conservation groups that aim to improve the environment and communities by making donations.

Voluntourism Programs
A few tour companies provide experiences that combine travel with worthwhile volunteer activities.

Cultural Experiences
Take part in regional cultural activities including customary dance, music, and crafts because they frequently assist local artisans.

Ecotourism Tours
Pick escorted excursions that have a focus on environmental preservation and offer enlightening information about Puerto Rico's distinctive ecosystems.

You may contribute to Puerto Rico's natural beauty and the wellbeing of its residents by adopting sustainable travel habits, choose eco-friendly lodgings, volunteering, and supporting regional initiatives. Respect, gratitude, and giving back to this wonderful island should be the themes of your journey.

Appendix

Useful Phrases In Spanish

When traveling to Puerto Rico, knowing some basic Spanish phrases can enhance your experience and help you communicate with locals. Here are some useful phrases:

1. Hello - Hola
2. Good morning - Buenos días
3. Good afternoon - Buenas tardes
4. Good evening - Buenas noches
5. Please - Por favor
6. Thank you - Gracias
7. Yes - Sí
8. No - No
9. Excuse me / I'm sorry - Perdón / Disculpe
10. Where is...? - ¿Dónde está...?
11. How much is this? - ¿Cuánto cuesta esto?
12. Can you help me? - ¿Me puede ayudar?
13. I don't understand - No entiendo
14. Restroom - Baño
15. Cheers! - ¡Salud!

Emergency Contacts and Medical Information

In case of emergencies while in Puerto Rico, here are important contact numbers and medical information:

1. General Emergency: 911
2. Puerto Rico Tourism Company: +1 (787) 721-2400
3. Medical Emergency: 911
4. Hospital / Ambulance: Dial 911 or go to the nearest hospital.
5. Police: 911
6. American Embassy in Puerto Rico:
   Address: 170 Federico Costa Street, San Juan, PR 00901
   Phone: +1 (787) 289-7088

Public Holidays and Festivals Calendar

To make the most of your trip, it's good to be aware of the public holidays and festivals in Puerto Rico.

Note that some businesses may be closed or have different operating hours during these times. Here are some major holidays and festivals:

1. New Year's Day - January 1
2. Three Kings' Day (Día de Reyes) - January 6
3. Martin Luther King Jr. Day - Third Monday in January
4. Presidents Day - Third Monday in February
5. San Juan Bautista Day - June 24
6. Independence Day - July 4
7. Constitution Day - July 25
8. Discovery of Puerto Rico Day - November 19
9. Thanksgiving - Fourth Thursday in November
10. Christmas Day - December 25

Puerto Rico is also known for its vibrant festivals, such as:

1. San Sebastián Street Festival (Fiestas de la Calle San Sebastián) - January
2. Casals Festival (Festival Casals) - February/March
3. Ponce Carnival (Carnaval de Ponce) - February/March
4. Saborea Puerto Rico - April
5. National Puerto Rican Day Parade - June (In New York City)

Made in the USA
Monee, IL
08 December 2023

48677537R00035